She Is

Michelle Scally Clarke

route

Michelle Scally Clarke

Michelle Scally Clarke is a performer
and poet from Chapeltown, Leeds.
She Is is her second book, her first
book, *I Am*, was published in 2001.

First Published by Route
PO Box 167, Pontefract, WF8 4WW
e-mail: books@route-online.com
web: www.route-online.com

ISBN: 1 901927 22 9

Cover Image:
Kevin Reynolds
www.kevinreynolds.co.uk

Cover design:
Andy Campbell
www.digitalfiction.co.uk

Support
Ian Daley, Isabel Galan, Roger Green, Roisin O'Shea,
Aerron Perry, Gerry Potter, Joe Williams, Nicole
Zepemeisel

Printed by Bookmarque, Croydon

A catalogue for this book is available
from the British Library

Route is an imprint of ID Publishing
www.id-publishing.com

She Is was produced thanks to support from the
Arts Council of England

For Joseph and Olivia and Shawn

She is – a moving walking she-woman ride, for she is an emotion, a passion, a warmth or a loss in every woman. *She is* – not of *me* but of *we*. My sisters, my mothers, my friends and our lovers, our joys and our struggles.

As a child I used to go skimming with my dad - drop a pebble in a stream and watch the ripple circle effect. Those circles are my story. There are no middles or ends to my story. Not dead yet! There is no right or wrong in this part of my journey, just a naked acceptance of what is. This is *she is*. Learning, growing, receiving and giving.

This book is a freedom. This book is a deeper kind of grace. I have my canvas now. A pattern to my walk, my fall, my loss, love and embrace. I have this, for in me, is *she*.

Insignificant changes

...my Irish grandmother was a farmer, so was my Nevis grandmother. They both lived by the sea and in my dreams I can see their market places. I can feel my ancestors pitch their stalls and sell their crops of mangoes and potatoes.

I never left the market, I was always there, pitching my voices. I'm always there, beckoning the audience to buy my wares.

Sold

The matches stare up at me -
'Ever had text with a stranger?'
Sex sells and I have sold myself
See I'm sat in a pub
Trying to avoid the dentist drill
Root painful canal surgery on my teeth
After my third JD it all seems simple to me
I have sold myself
When I have finished this addictive liquid
I will mingle among the mid-afternoon crowd
Go to Morrisons, shop for tea
Hoping the bright snazzy labels
Don't 'more reason' me
Don't jump out too much, attract, tempt
And touch me
To sell myself
This is a futile drive
Where no one is that good
And nice is as common as rice
I'll pick from the apple tree
Just like Eve
Quick fixes I need
I am weak
And I sell myself
When I fly into the orbit of me
When I sing and dance poetry
When I'm potent, sexual, human and free
I'll sell myself

Lots of beautiful insignificant changes happening round me. My life is up to me. I can now stand those mothers in the playground who assume I'm a half-wit, half-awake. For it's me that has to struggle to raise my housing rent, trying not to worry all the time. No class for me, no box with a tick, no credit cards or financial security. And the clock moves differently from nine till five, I'm in a train half my life - giving, bearing and sharing a smile. Strong and yet I'm weak, I'm moving along.

Beautiful

The beautiful insignificance of being a mother
Til someone asks you
How they are
Then the beauty of them
Strikes in your heart
Every touch of them, renew the cells
Every cry from them, burns like hell
Accepting defeat to give harder
Gifts from the highest order
And yet they come along
And teach you to rediscover
Yourself
For in you
And of you
Born of you
And raised
They will go their own way
Bigger than yesterday
More confusing than today
With the beautiful insignificance
They feel on their way

Goodbye friend. What's your name again friend?
(Dirty laugh) Wish you well, friend. Who can tell
when we'll talk again? I've got over what I threw
over. Have found my legs again to stumble into
my future, thank you!!

Lost memory

Lost my memory
When I left you
Though
I never really had you
Did I, Honey?
It wasn't in the sigh of pleasure
That escaped without trace

I could never really
Have held you
Charmed by my story
Rich and bitter in taste
And the grass was long and green homey
As you trampled the bridge to the other side
And my memory seems to escape me
Darling
Did you hold me enough?
Until my last tear dried
And I'm all alone now, homey
Central heating broke
And I'm cold inside
Seems you took my honey, homey
And gagged when the sweetness stung your pride
I lost my memory
Did I give you my love to break in two
I should have really waited
But I'm fast
Longed for the scent of one and one makes two
And the grass was long and green and lush,
Homey
As you waded past my hurt
To my love and perfume
Guess I got it into my head, lover
That this thing would last
Most lovers do
Lost my memory

It's always a good day when the sun shines down, you can catch a smile in an eye. Walking down my avenue I caught a blessing for myself. Feeling grown - feeling alive - feeling woman. The shame and anger have been replaced. The baggage thrown away, my thinking and feeling are in harmony. Starting to look at things in peace...head flung high.

She knows now

Flung head held high
Strolling on
She knows now
Can't walk under clouds
Needing light to raise thoughts
Turning to grace
She knows now

Basic needs, oxygen from trees
Blessing their lines of majesty
Growing to maturity
Raised by their energy
Always been tougher
Bigger than she
She knows now
Life does not always look the same
Fire is in joy
A different colour from colour
From lain sleeping in negativity
Passion musk and compost heap
England is like English weather
Today she dressed for it
Walked these same stones these roads
Now holding her chakra in tight
To tummy through her child
Till the veins hold her spine
For her ancestors climb
Smile through darkness into light
Seek an' she will find
She knows now
The habit of hurt is falling roun'
Love not afraid to catch
The reflection of I
Head flung high
She knows now

Lust is all well and good and not to be mistaken for love, which I did. So I gave and gave and he took it away, leaving, not to give back. And, in hindsight, so he should. If you offered me cake on a plate I'd eat it!!!!!!

A pretty male energy vampire, a girl in love with love and the sex was good, at first, 'til the aggressive demands got out of hand and giving blow jobs hurt. I had to realise too - in all my demise - that I'd sat him in my place to begin with.

After

After I fucked him
After I loved him
After I fed him
After I forgave him
After I 'lowed him
After he sat in my chair
Eating my space
After I found the silence
That the back of his back
Could only bring
Did I pick up myself
In my pen
Was I free to be me
In me again

An old lonely woman passed by and as our
shadows crossed she flashed her bluest of blue
eyes at me, then walked away. But, in between
that space, her sadness and reality knocked on
my day, in the face. Shook to the core I turned
my eyes from her, but that blue of her eyes
followed me, followed me in my mind and I felt to
write of her and remember her. Is it fear that
stops tomorrow? Is it your reflection or mine
that make us avert our eyes? I can't remember if
I smiled, hope I tried.

Issues

I try not to see myself in her ways
Everyday searching the dustbins
To find yesterday's dinner
For tomorrow's evening meal
I hide
Cover my hands to my eyes
Like a child I pretend to be invisible
And as I turn each corner
I see her laden with her weight
Of bags and old jumpers
Vexed down by her groundhog days
Unable to walk or stop
Heaving her world upon her shoulders
She pretends to be invisible
Cusses and snides hide her eyes
We both know
She cannot see tomorrow

'You see you, you're just a woman you are.'
That's what he said.

Ego rises to fight one another. The shattered
self bawls out a volcano of words you can't
take back. You feel the slice of your tongue.
Harm inflicted.

In the still

I'm in the still
Of angry embers
Soothing red fires
Flames turning
From golden to blue
Just before
Just before dying
Gone

I'm in the ego
Of demon tongue
An' fist a flying
Knocking out and destroying
Just before
Just before dying
Gone

I'm in the peace
That's forever trying
Soothing to spitting
Tigers and kittens
Tough love
Of the lone she-lion
Walking alone
Walking alone
Gone

The cold that let in the rain

I always perceived them as strong women but today, I don't know what the word 'strong' means. Addiction is a big word and yet, as I speak of others, I too am addicted - just to different poison.

It bit, when you fell in front of me, sister. When I had to pick you up, your cover-up brought up fear. Had I taken on too much?

Footsteps

Your footsteps still blaze your trail
Yet in another way
Could weep every time without fail
For your possession is real
It's on your face
Startled yet denying
There is something wrong
So as I pick up my pen
With humbleness and jus' in case
You remember we young
But we old in these ways

You full of crack, queen
It's on your back
Attacking your genius
With bullshit crap

What broke for you, sister
What made you give up
Were the demons in your head
Shouting too much?
So many years now, sister
You won worn down for today
Your footsteps blaze your trail, mama
Jus' in another way

Weep I weep for us, ghost mother
Love gets stronger everyday
But I dare come no closer
It's too dark in there to play

Have you ever had that feeling that you have just experienced someone else's journey? If it was mine, then I've been there before and I can't ignore my lessons. I have lived my world with the punch and the backhand, not over and over, but more often than. Now it wasn't my turn. I jumped in to save my friend from attack. One backhand and the room turns black.

Worth

She has gained worth
I'm putting an assumption
On her birth
For when she dies
She'll give back to the earth
After been knocked down
Beaten down, broken crown
The spirit still rises
Before his hands went roun'
Her neck
I'm a man
He said
You'd best not forget
I'm a man
He said
Knocking her to the floor

I'm a man
He said
An' hurt her more
Til she felt like dirt
In his slaps
Til she did not cover herself
And fight back
I'm the man
He said
Then she snapped
After too many years of attacks
She laughed
I'm a woman
She said
Your mother was a woman too
I'm a woman
She said
And I hurt just like you
I'm a woman
She said
In my love
In my flaws
And as my spirit rises
Yours sinks to the floor

There's no fears in physical pain for me these
days, just a wariness of the anger and the danger
of the hurt. All damaged people and all their
damaged days learning nothing, she is on his
hand.

The cold that let in the rain

When her brother kissed her
She knew he really loved her
While trembling undercover
Praying for day
Now she's much older
She does not see her brother
And blocks the distant memories
The ones that cause the pain
At length she could not remember
When she first discovered
Her pattern to woman, hide
The rhythm that let in the rain

Well you call her a sinner
Cry her a river
She'll play the sinner for you

She had many men as lovers
As beaters and as brothers
She became the fire night cracker
The first person to play
Alcohol became her lover
Make-up her cover
To slap on the mask
And to roar with the pain

Well you call her a sinner
Cry her a river
She'll play the sinner for you

So they told her it was cancer
That was eating her liver
Her spirit inside shrieked
'Could you love me some today?'
And the bed she tried to cover
The make-up and the lovers
Broke the bank to her river
Broke the dam to her pain

Well you call her a sinner
Cry her a river
She'll play the sinner for you

I'm not the one to say sorry for her harm. I'm
just here to love her. I don't know if she wanted
ever to escape from her fright. He kept her as
pure as a child and sometimes she'd let you hear
the siren of her cry, not loud like her streets, her
men or her clothes, but lost in the purgatory of
that little girl.

Safe

She, a child, felt safe in your arms
But you changed all of that
Grown up fragile strong beauty
She knew memories would last
Good or bad
The skies an' the stars
Lit your fate
The wind bound you together
In the cold and the rain
Then you changed all of that
With your fear and wrath
She gave to you
Wanting it to find you whole
Lay with you, each driving
In different zones
Such a lonely soul
In the abuse you call love
What was she running to
Your love or your punch
She, a woman, tries to feel safe in your arms
You try to change all of that
With your love and your wrath
Grown up fragile beauty
She knows memories last
Good or bad

My niece came, bad day to my house. Said my brother, her dad, was in the crack house an' he's not coming out. He's falling into the pipe tin. I hear, but can't feel nothing. Guess I wanted to hide, wanted to reach for the drink. Maybe I felt justified or maybe cos I too lost in the lie. I could tell by her eyes.

She is mine. I know what she's been thru. I cannot step in, but sit and watch the waves of destruction flow on her, yet never crash her down. Humble is her grace, she is a beautiful soul in a storm without a coat.

Her cooking pot remains dirty on the stove, her life is that of the clock awaiting his return, hands kisses and fists, back track promises, veiled eyes that make her want to rock and cry.

It's so sad that such a big hearted woman that you are, can't love yourself, to see the gifts that are waiting.

I wrote a poem on my mother's birthday but it was not for her, it's for my birth-mother. When I teach poetry I ask people to clean out their closets. I can see I was cleaning mine.

Gems

Ran away
To another man
Another rum, another punch
Til income

Couldn't tell her child
That diamond drops
Shone in her afro hair
Couldn't find her voice
Through rage and despair
Tried to tell the world
Her hatred for life
Through her bottles through her
Bruises
Through chaos and sacrifice

Run away
To another man
Another rum another punch
Til income
So she ran away
With a different man
Another bed, kick in the head
Til she done

Just so angst
Twisted torn by
Life's bitter knife
Could not show for her mother
By her graveside
Gulped back the liquor
Til it burnt inside
Her hate, a cloak, darkened her life

So she ran away
To another man
Another rum another punch
Til she done
(have to get away)

Hope her children can see
The diamonds they leave behind
Hope addiction does not fix
On the fragileness of our line
Did she love her children to their very grain
Could she see at all from deep within her pain

Run away
To another man
Another rum another punch
Til she dead

Is there a space for everything? If there is then
this is just one of those circles that seems to go
nowhere and, I guess, I wrote it on my mother's
birthday because the contrast between both
women is sharper, in my life, than a line of good
poetry.

Banging my head in the dark

Little birds in the trees
Is life as tough for you as for me?
Don't feel like I've
Had no peace
Just pulls and demands
Stress and needs
I'm banging my head in the dark
Banging my head in the dark
I'm banging my head in the dark
Banging my head
In the dark

Lost to the sense
Of this disillusioned time
Beware you can't see me
You lost your sight
Moving through a head space of time
Don't pick me up
It's cruel to be nice
I'm banging my head in the dark
Banging my head in the dark
Banging my head
In the dark

Some big force
Needs to birth this out
Transcend these weights
And shout it all about
Somewhere I can hear my song
It goes just like
A ding a ling a ling a long long
I'm banging my head in the dark
Banging my head in the dark
Banging my head
In the dark

And I can't talk 'bout dancing
Cos no one's taking me
What's the use
Of imagining there was going to be
So I sit in silence
Flicking the TV
Losing myself to its hypocrisy
And I'm banging my head in the dark
Banging my head in the dark
Banging my head
In the dark

All is stress mummy......... Bang bang bang
Feel worn out again mummy.... Bang bang bang
Monday soon come mummy weekend slipped by
birds still sing in the trees
Another year flies by ....all is stress, same old
test, single mummy ....Bang bang bang

Lust took me by the hand and I agwan with my
wanton ways and ego filled haze...oh, I let you
sweet talk me again but I seen you walking by,
day after day how you laughed with your sons,
how gentle your ways and in fantasy, in lonely
summer days, I developed a crush. My energy
preyed on you and you took my demands gentle
with quiet glee and I fell too soon.

Let's put it down to sexual needs and touching
hands, skin on skin communication. I'd been a
long time without a man or even a hug from
stronger arms, stronger than me but not as
weak.

It wasn't just a one-night stand

It wasn't just a one-night stand
Was it?
Though you'd be pressed to understand
My need to be held by a man
You being a man who loves woman
I didn't just give myself away on a plate
Did I?
You had so much
You filled your face
Your eyes too big for After Eights
Can't you make more room
Fit me in
I didn't open a can of worms
Did I?
To all my fears
Still have to learn
To walk not run
Be still stay strong.....

It wasn't just a one-night stand
Was it?

A beautiful friend told me to write a letter to
God. She told me to write down what I seek in
union. Am I in love with love?

Dear God

Dear God,
As you know, 'cause you're great
That in my loneliness I often make mistakes
The feel and touch of sex
And carnal knowledge to be love
And for that I now know myself
I know God that you love me at every encounter
When I am enslaved
When I am passioned and addicted
I know you are there, that is not my problem.
My problem dear God is love
and the pure truth of it
Am I being fed of lies?
Contained and shrunk to fear of society?
God help me please.
Dear God please could I meet a man who can sail
my boat, through waves of tranquillity
A man to give space and take space.
I need to give my love
Tired of the one-night stands and
faceless demands
I wait as the universe answers my prayers

Wake

Been in a crash? That mad! Not our General?

Sat at Miriam's house. Can't seem to let the
words seep in. Have a feeling that I'm dead as
well. Felt like I was just listening in.

He's dead. The world stops still.
Can't catch my breath. Scared to.

Wake

Blessings rain bittersweet grief
Photographs pass a tear moving picture
Tears fall in heart attack
You're not coming back
Friend

Slow to recover
Feel old before time
Sharp as the weather cuts still your smile
Bills still come in
After you dead
You always said
Friend

Friendship is a beautiful thing. In life and in death
General gives me love. I'm a passenger of pain.
Memories hold deep in the membranes, the pull-
out strands of beautiful fibres full of love and
fun. I pause and I reflect on the hard and difficult
days when words were exchanged, but in
friendship like family we became.

How I looked up to him cos I was his sister.

It was General's funeral today and calm descended on me as I woke. I had the most important job to do for my best friend, I had to send him off and lay his body in the ground. I had to be as strong as he and hold his child and comfort his family. I had to rise and speak at church, speak the poem that myself and his stepdaughter wrote to the mass of family and the world of friends. There were so many races gathered in his name sharing our love for him, releasing the pain and it hurt.

Catch your smile

An' most times you praise them
As you stand in their family grace
An' all the love General showed us
Was sun upon our face
And to catch your smile in your
Tia's face
Is the blessing through you when
No one there to hold your place

I can still remember you said to me in November
when I asked if your family knew I was your
family too. 'Truly' you said 'if I die you'll be riding
with my family in the car'.
'That's alright' I said and we laughed.
Fate, truth came thru thou in the jest.

Today I felt years older than me. It was like my
labours in its intensity and love of my soul. I felt
old but privileged. I met General when I was just
fourteen, I never knew we'd have a friendship 'til
the end. That's why I had to do today right, one
of the most beautiful bittersweet important days
of my life.

Always a worker, always broke, always buy you a brandy and orange and pick up your woes. He left nothing but his richness, his love for one love testimony. In his death he taught me love was his greatest attribute. This is my will.

Will

Will the blackbirds and sun shine for me
When I close my final eye
Will you read my poetry
As you tell them of my smile
Just remember the light in me
The playmate and the life
My love for forget-me-not blue skies
My love for Hayfield night
Will you read my words eloquently
As in life you treat my soul
Do not forget my children's tears
For I am in their bones
Lay me in the earth
Beneath a willow tree
An' laugh as you explain
I was sometimes melancholy

On his death his prophecy rang true for he left
the church rammed, the street rammed,
Roundhay Road was blocked off. I could not see
for the faces but guess I knew almost the lot.

My history and landmarks are being pulled down.
Places where I'd spent my youth and discovered
my roots. Chapeltown is changing. The Hayfield
gone. The Hayfield was an old diva of a building
and, in my dad's day, a sharp and happening place
to go dancing, you had to be suited and booted,
looking fine.

Hayfield

In the rumble of the ghetto
In the scrape of metal
To concrete floor
The breathing of the crane
As it eats sicks and gores
The Hayfield's down
It's really coming down
The sky shows its dismay
In a dark an' grey
There's a pain in my chest
For yesterday days
Well, there no Mr Joof's
There no Silvertree
No rhythms no blues
Well there's no Hayfield
No vinyl playing
Reminding we are free
Just cultures and vultures
Pop Idol on TV

Chapeltown coming like a crack town
All the bars have been shot down

There's a fire burning in the Hayfield ground
They're tearing down
Yes they're pulling it down
Pulling down all
Her history
Good and bad

Where are the elderly to pass things on
Where has all the music gone
Where is the joy and the gaiety
Lost to the drugs of fear an' greed
Lost to the words of hyprocisy
Lost to emotions without no keys

Goodbye to the General
My treasured friend
A trove of memories in my chest
For the old community
We lost we got
Blessed are the one's that know
In this pay an' go
In this dash an' throw
Hold tight please

Leeds town, is my birth town
Where the community found
Can cleanse and breathe
The community on the ground
Chant up and plea
Cos the Hayfield down
It's really coming down
The sky shows its dismay
In a dark and grey
There's a pain in my chest
For yesterday days
Give back to our mentors
Who talk with clarity
Give back to all the peoples

Who walk in sincerity
Give back the words of wisdom to the old
Give back to the joy that the youth can invoke
Give back to the joy in the community
Let it breathe. Let it breathe
In the words of Martin Luther King
'I have a dream!'

I found Chapeltown at the age of fourteen and I
met with a community. I could breathe, go wild
and dance, there was a time to flee and a time to
come back to heal. And the time I have now to
grow back the seed for the core that has fed me,
supported my dreams.

This is for the young forgotten kids in prison, paying for society's mistakes. It's for all the forgotten, the silent who scream, the young soldiers on the politicians' war fields, dying from the guns that we paid for; the mothers, children, sons and loved ones, innocent civilians. The orphans and carers, the old and the poor, single parents struggling, fearing bailiffs at their door. This is for the illiterate, the genius who hustles cos he's been told nothing good. This is for when they laugh, this is for when we sing, this is for the strength of human spirit.

Somewhere

Somewhere over the reignbow
Is the forgotten you leave behind
There you'll find me dancing
Swinging on my lullabies

I was born in a thousand heavens
Watched while you teef my stars
You sat me down in a desert
I created oasis out of Jupiter and Mars
You tried to stop my heart bass
See me skipping with my skipping rope
Whilst we belly laugh through hunger
Strange fruit still rot and choke

Somewhere over the reignbow
Is the forgotten you leave behind
There you'll find us dancing
Swinging on our lullabies

Witness of your blood
Bored by your greed carnage and anger
Does our smile disturb your plan
Or the space you take from roun' us
As we breathe with our children

I gave you my son
Watch you charge for his moon
But we laughin' now
We feel we cry

Distant but distinct
In the milkyway night
I gave you a fresh bud
Watched your silent screamed face
For you dared to see me blossom
For it hurt to see my grace

Somewhere over the reignbow
Is the forgotten you leave behind
There you'll find we dancing
Swinging on our lullabies
Ghetto style

I was working in a prison today, trying to reach lads who have been scared and taught not to look within, so that memories become crimes as they rot inside. I talk with them of my own beat, the dub that holds my heart and craves my soul. I tell of my journey, my stories. Then I ask them theirs and to tell them truthfully and with the emotion they felt, then and there. Truth comes from everyone in their different heartbeat and, if judgement is left aside, then the soul can but meet and listen and heal.

My hurting feels like a sea of cancer and some days I am loathe to do my best because we're all going to die of something, whether we chose it or it was deemed. Feels like I'm fighting the distraction all day long.

The mass of destruction sent to us, the spin of witches' lies, the fear that is constructed to maim is the cancer in our food for thought.

Cancer rap

Can you take back your
Satellites, guns, and MTV?
Take back your computers
Your billions an' greed
Can you put back the diamonds
Rebuild the crust of the earth
Can you stop with your war games?
This is time for peace and love

Can you feed all our people
From the table of western greed
Can you take back the crack an' get off our back
Remove the Big Mac
'Cos I'm not lovin' the obesity

Can you take off the debt
For the first to be free
Can you vaccinate all from
HIV
Can you stop the fragile
Being cruise missiled
On TV
Cause you feed us
Cancer from the hypocrisy
You lie then you lie to the first degree
The blind man
Is a wake man and the wake
Man is asleep
Credit thrown at us
We in debt too deep
Rainforests been mashed
To fulfil our needs
While poverty keeps
Rising the cat got the
Cream, take back the
Saucer, take back your crap
Take back your bushfire
And come off we backs!!!!

It is the 23rd of December. Time moves on and then stops. Today was a bad day. I am mourning my friend on the anniversary of death. The weather's a slap in the face. Sharply turning down Briggate I am faced in the rain by the throng like a fog of people with pinched faces, as mine.

I hated shopping today. I really can't stand the pushing aggressive shopping frenzied charm of last minute Christmas shoppers, sweating and leaking drops of rain. Shops, space, Leeds town, western towns groaning, with the chorus of neon-timed alarmed jingles that make me want to run back home.

Present ghost

Mass of glitter lights
I keep on walking
A fusion wailing present ghost
Baubles tinsel stars illuminate
This 24/7 hour western race

The dark nights are colder
Than I remember
Santa now looks evil
Necking Coke
Deck the walls with
Neon-nosed reindeers
A tacky destiny
Dressed in red robes

They have cancelled Christmas
In Bethlehem
Thousands of lives
Lost in Jesus' home
Gather your kin
Closer to yer
Remember all that glitters
is not quite gold

I am feeling so needy today. I have had the whole of female power around me and what have I done? Fallen into my well. I crave some human touch today. I want to hear somebody call me 'Baby'. I want my friend back, who can glance his glance and then we laugh and every time so free in flight he comes right back to me.

It's funny how loss touches you and leaves you breathless, sucked out, winded and confused. It strips you down, leaving you feeling alone in the core. All my needs come rising like cream and I feel to scream - somebody help me please or hold me, give me a quick lift so I can forget the hurt like this. It's funny how the loss of my friend and the need for physical touch come out attached to each other. Loss makes us want to fuck, fuck up loads or just fuck off.

I'm on in my therapy of the page. I'm in the primary loss of touch and sometimes it hurts too much.

Deep waters

It's been a year now
And though I still sing my song
It hurts sometimes
Don't feel like I've left something
Behind
I don't know if it's the age
That kills us or the pain
No shallow waters
I'm fleeing to deep rivers
How you raised me
How we walked
Side by side always a smile
Everything you gave in me General
There's nothing of you
That I'll leave behind

She is

I spent the night with Nina Simone, kids in bed, I home alone. I felt her soul liquidate my bones, releasing a calm, cooling my nerves. She sang for me out of the CD. Only for she I wept with relief. I found you, I screamed in the night and then we laughed and then we jived. Was ever a time that I felt so free, so near to God, so near to me?

She

Got the whole world in her hand
Got the maps and the atlas on her back
Is human woman good and bad?
Got the whole world in her hands

Got the power of inspiration in her hand
Got no money by Wednesday
Dem making demands
Got the whole world in her hands

An' the court and the bailiffs
Dem making demands
The water and taxman making demands
Got the babies of her babies, in her hands
Got the whole world in her hands
And she's juggling like crazy
To all the demands, as the televised
Nation watches the lottery of bombs
All the mothers and their babies
In red-night vision
Got the whole world in her hands

How many tongues can I speak? How many lovers will I meet? How many of my children will I see fly the nest? How many times will I face my tests?

Today it does not matter for I've woken with that feeling - gwan girl you're doing good and so what life has to throw me today I'll catch and throw it back, because today I feel my power, people. There's no turning back.

I know this woman

I know this woman
Called me
Who in Dutch Courage days
Gets what she says
Can catch her man
Or throw him away

I know this woman
Called me
Can catch a glad days
Give pure thanks and praise
For the glory of joy
And to feel it

I know this woman
Called me
Who loves all she can
In the spirit of human
And hate ain't got no room
To see

I love my children. It is one thing that is easy, it's everything else that you juggle. They juggle society's hustle and there are no easy lessons. I am blessed by the forgiveness of my children, am blessed in the rush of love that flows to the touch every time we are together. My soul triangle - my boy, my girl and me all born on the eighteenth. This is my gift from God, the greatest works of all.

Be

When my daughter was born
I was as new as she
The black of her
The black of my skin
Sang and shone joy
An' morning had broken
When I lifted my daughter
From between my legs
Bit her umbilical cord
And put her to my breast
I knew what I was
And who I would be

When my son was born
I was only nineteen
Fresh and green and full of need
I suckled him with my whole
As he fed of body
And I found in him all of my sanctuary
For I knew what we were
And who we'd be

I've been running for so many years. It's only looking back now that I can see that I'm woman, I am she is. I am mother and the weight of that kept me in denial as a young girl, a young child. Denials allowed me to wear the robes of bitch and whore and I wore my insecure feathers like a poncho around my neck. I raged at my mother, wanting her to be perfect and yet feeling her perfect made me feel like shit, so I threw it at her and never missed.

Looking in to my teenagers' eyes I see the struggle and how they want to run from my nagging voice that dishes out chores and not much else. I see it when they've had a bad day at school then dance on me like I'm the fool and then I'm the emotional punch-bag catching my child's feelings and making them see glad. I've stopped and looked around and I see my mother in my hands, in my flaws, for she is my rise and now I am my fall for, I am mother.

She is

Did you run away as a little girl
Can you see her when you look into her walls
She's on your hands
She's your flaws
She's your rise
She's your fall

Worse than a period pain
Or panther claw
She rips out your heart
Then she'll come back for more
Enters your body
Leaves from your pores
She is warm fat raindrops
On volcanic fall

She is light
The softness you held
As a child
She is your wombliss
Your womb man blitz
Then you dis
Then you bitch
Then you dis dis dis
She is
The smell of your pillow
When you wake up in morn
She gets into your body
And comes out of your pores
When you fear
When you rape
When you call her a whore
She's your mother
She's your very first smile

Did you run away as a little girl?
Can you see it when you look into her walls
She's on your hands
She's your flaws
She's your rise
She's your fall
She is your mother

Here it comes, that loss thing, that separated at birth (it was a good thing too). Love gets stronger everyday, though I have not said your name, the way I think of you has changed for the time being. I've let you go free, not fearful of your shadows I thought I couldn't flee.

Womb

She is my mother
She is a ghost
Born in her blood
Birthed from her womb
She is........gone
I cannot remember
She is.........myself
I often wonder
Or is she my daughter
She is my enemy
In self abusive anger
She is........lost love

Am I whole
Just to let go
Do I have a choice
What is my role
Do I know love
Could I let it go
She is my mother

Gone – yesterday
Her birthday
My let-off day
A day to celebrate her journey
Or was it a nightmare?
For I am here
My children carry the blood
My blood born in blood
What is love
She is
She is forgiven

I went to see a clairvoyant and she told me that
I'd met my mother in the garden before I was
born and that we'd talked. Do you believe in that
stuff? I think I do and anyway it's been a comfort
to lay down something and let it go, yet if I'm
really honest, I don't know if I'm ready to know
her truth.

In the garden

We met in the garden before I was born
There she gave me the tools of her soil
Before her fall, (autumn, winter, fall)
October born
One was for courage
Help face the days
One was for stubbornness
To keep truth in my ways
And I guess Mary was there
Guiding her through
For I understand then and now
That I'll never know you
Send her the angels
Take her from hell
To love and renew her children cells
Where is my Ireland
Where is my home
It's back in the garden
Before I was born

Rejection, abandonment, fear and loss
War, self mental anguish,
The devil's own plot
But he's not in our story, mother
No not today, even though you have
Died to me, I'll put flowers on your grave
For to be in anger, for to be distressed
For to be forgotten and lost
Was not as a child you
Longed for
But you got

I saw her pictured in my head today and she was
just a child. In the same path as her, would I have
walked her mile? I got a second rush of warmth.
When I thought to the love I call mother, how I
have fought her and depressed her, how I made
her my birth-mother's pillow and in that split
second you know what I wished? That my birth-
mother had a mother as good as me, the woman
who adopted, cherished and nurtures me thru my
role as a mother and my loss of you.

Turkey stuffing

Christmas is here again, two years on from the last days of seeing General's smile. But you know what, it feels alright.

In comes Sammi with a bottle of wine, the Christmas shopping done, we start to unwind. I open the wine, chatting and gasping, killing it laughing, healing and freeing up stress from within. Then Sammi asked what I wanted in my destiny and in the spirit of the lasses of Chapeltown, Yorkshire, I ask for a man I could walk with and rise with proper. It seems like I'm always for man doesn't it? But I'd had months and months of habitation. A new change, a fresh page and a special General watching over me.

Destiny

Destiny, shine a little light on me
Maybe
I've been all the good woman I can be
So come and shine your
Smile, tonight

Destiny, I picked up my flower
An' I sowed my seed, recognised the
Garden and the cartwheel
So come and blitz me open tonight

Destiny, I'm so fulfilled
But my body's so lonely
To give the joy of my pleasure
My love, my being
Beneath a freedom beneath the stars

Destiny, come on, find a gentle man for me
A sweet, freed, kind of fun with
Liberty
And hurry, hold my senses tonight

I am not desperate for the man, cos I can't see him. Have had brief glimpses of him, in all sorts of man. All together, the whole package looks far off. And anyway, me and the girls have been working hard on ourselves, on our studies and careers with our kids and I'm feeling alright about being sat round my table talking to the ladies.

Sammi opens with one of her journeys and the table blows up, the leering and saucing, squawking and bawling, bubbling over like a pan sick on the stove...and the man...the man got told. Pure golden day fun.

Charlatan man

Her hot self must have
Blown up in a foolish man's eyes
A promise made in comfort
To a woman's sad cries
You make her feel icky picky
Drop down on the floor
She's going to show
Your tricky dicky
She's so much more

You carried so much baggage
She must be a fool
She must be so foolish
You cannot live your rule

You were born with a willy
She was born with a womb

What's all this 'new man' shit?
You cave-man lord
You as pretty as your peacock
You as shallow as you small
She means that in all ways
You upset her talk
Dance your player's game
While she remove her form

What's all this noise about?
When it's there
You fraud
You say she the only one
In your future talk
Then you diss her
Back off
And fraud
Too many sweets in the sweetie shop
You ready to gorge

You were born with the willy
Me were born with the womb
If we can get it together now
You'll see it's oh so cool
You'll see it's all so cool!!

I am rediscovering myself in my thirties in my peak. Feels better than twenties as the valleys are not so steep. My palette is changing, my skin maturing, my belly wrinkling and frowning, and blemishing maps from where I have been. The fading stretch marks that line my legs and breast, my dark brown nipples large proud and erect, the curve of my backside, the eczema that comes and goes, the sheath and colours of my skin that covers my bones.

Turkey stuffing

I jus want a man for Christmas time
A man to hold me close
A man to tell me how sexy my backside is
A man, to drown in myself
And it runs to new years day
Then I can say it's meant to last
For though the turkey stuffing taste great
It goes off pretty fast
I jus' want a man for my birthday
Who can wake me on the day
With buttered toast dripping
As he undresses me to my toes
Who big-UPs the children as
I tear open their surprise
I jus' wan a man with freedom
A man who lives out his lot
Who'll put his possessions down
To travel and get lost
If I was a man that's where
I'd be, wandering lost and totally free

I'm rediscovering my sensuality without a 'guilty'
or 'I'll get catch' as I fiddle with my rabbit
praying the batteries will last. (Attention all
ladies if you don't know what a rabbit is then a
very nice lady called Anne Summers does.
Empowerment and safe sex, at least it's a sure
come!)

I was six when I was adopted. I was eleven by the time I picked up my eldest sister's flute. Annie's flute. I have been given and I've played, I have fought and strayed. Being given something so beautiful placed fear in me, I didn't believe in beauty. Thought it was a trick and dissed it. Now I found my own page and am amazed by the music I was given.

Adopting

Picking up the flute
I was not aware
Of how it was meant to be
How I would struggle to breathe
In a key that didn't call my name
I felt clumsy and quick
Sometimes awkward and sick
When the notes came out wrong
And my fingers didn't belong
I practised every day
Memorising myself to play
I found in a breath in a note
A releasing energy
Something I made
Something in me
I played every day
Growing confident

Reading
Notes on the page
Then I turned of age
An' the flute still played
'Lithely an' liberally'
Nothing said
On my skin I still felt
Its keys calling out
For harmony
Choking me up with
Rage
Put the flute away
It calling my name
Needed drum and bass
Overcome with pipe of peace
In my war and rage
Let it go for
In one of those days
Lost my space
And in blinking disgrace
Forgot what the notes
Were played for
Still the flute stayed
Til I'd found my way
Nowadays
It holds my grace
We are on the same page
Picking up the flute
My fingers dance on the keys
Thanking and praising
Fluently breathing

Tonight I sat round my beautiful family, sat in peace. Our Christmas started out with my wanting to go to midnight mass. I knew I wanted my children to have a taste of my childhood Christmas, but there was more. I wanted to walk and face my loss in the church and for what it now stood for. Love for love comes from change, weakness, war and fall, it comes from crying and believing, healing and understanding self, saying thank you, I am here, how I truly belonged, today I came out of the box to be greeted and mothered for I am their child.

Circles

I took my children to midnight mass
My locks covered beneath my hat
We sat with my sister and parents in a pew
Near to the front, we had to be early
cos that Scally tradition
My ties and my bows, my new pretty clothes
All memories to share to my children's vision
So there we sat in the church
Giggling as usual slightly nervous, unrehearsed
An octave too high in all the Christmas carols
I looked and watched the priest an' his clan
The trainer priest
With his severe speech impediment

I came to the simple conclusion that love is love when it's let go with pure feeling. I can love anyone to the best I can, felt a joy inside me, I'll offer another chance. When there's no going back, love gives us courage with the widest roar, I feel a change through the next day, affirmations be in my breast, my pulse, in my hands, I give up my peace, my joy, my thanks.

Sat in the early morning hour
Presents wrapped under the tree
Love is in my tired hands
The children snore in their dreamlands
I take a break piece of space
To acknowledge you are here
God of begotten not created one god of this world and the mess we've made it. God who loves me in all my falls, the blessed energy that is within my grasp. To touch, to connect, to breathe at last.

The festival of tomorrow

Had a dream last night that I was in the car with my past and I wanted to get out but forgot how to shout. And me and my past never once laughed, just drove round and round trying to find a home. I woke up lost and had to soothe my fear lord down.

Today

Clear out the closet
Come out
Or get back in
Empty out your dustbins
There's so much rubbish
Piled in
Smile at in the lonely
Eyes
An' love yourself today
Dance naked in the rain
Laugh like you the clown
Share your goat from the dutchie pot
And pull your fences down
Sing till your lungs inflate
Fill your story, feel your page
Rejoice and celebrate
An' love yourself today

(Let go)

Lost baggage you never realised you hadn't picked up, didn't miss it again 'til love came your way. It's just I see a different kind of passionate and I'm all wrapped up in greens and blues and different tunes.

Just a likkle bit of madness, just a likkle bit of gold. When the drop of light hits you it invigorates your soul. Just a tinge of pure movement in the naked glimpse of light, a shadow that's all birthed you, in your words, in your flight. A likkle bit of trust, jus a smidgen of respect for the opposite sex, just a likkle bit of truth, just try it a little, what's to lose...?

Ya vie lublo[*]

With happy times I'll ground you
Dance round, with you, clown with you
With loving arms, surround you, hold you down
Try bring you round
I'll be your back of rock
Your biggest friend
Support you for being
Ya vie lublo
Ya vie lublo
I wasn't gonna use it myself til
I fell for you

[*] Ya vie lublo - 'I love you' in Russian, once said by
Steve McQueen.

Sisters

Milk an' honey offerings
I bring to thee
Flight in beauty
Orsia of sweet waters
Goddess of sensuality
Spirit inside of me
Orsia of sweet waters
Orsia of sweet waters

Sisters it's been a long time
Since I put you on my page
But do you remember the day
We placed our hands
Our feet
Our toes
To the cold of the waters

Goddess of sensuality
Spirit inside of me
Milk an' honey offers
I bring to thee
For your flight in beauty
Orsia of sweet waters
Orsia of sweet waters

Sisters it's been a long time
Since we been brave
An' in the innocence of the day
We gave ourselves away
As the man moved away
From the waters

Left by ourselves to discover
A baptism of pleasure
Streams through a rock
The visual treasures
Cities forgot
As we gave ourselves away
To the innocence of the day
And played
We played

Hope, hope, hope, I've got it back in my lungs and
I am ready to harvest hope. Find and face myself
for tomorrow, as naked as the child who refused
to put her clothes on. Today I will follow my will
and wake up from the deep sleep I've been hiding
in and cocooning myself within a growing spree,
new steps towards the unfolding me, a feast of
tomorrow.

The festival of tomorrow

Today is a day full of new dreams,
aspirations, harvests and hopes
Crops for tomorrow
A birth of full experience
A festival of light, dark and shade
And her weathered diaspora
Now a well-worn friend, this journey
Is the cobbles, her path to the very end
She will pick up the rice seeds to make a bead
A new an' old, the same recipe
The unspoken crown upon her head
A breath in which woman breathes
But forgets she has spoken
The binding of her choices and skills
In the motion of her children

Today she is as naked as the child
Who refused to put her clothes on
She is forgotten today she is free

Today she will pick up the mildew stone
With eyes as precious as she
Amongst the soil the leaves the rocks
To find out what she flees
She is the heart of a sea coral
Moss on a rock, Medea, Cleopatra
The single mother, raver, sinner
Red hot lover, pleasure giver, storyteller,
Her story she maketh
The abuser of self and the abused of others
Not confused, no right or wrong
My friends this journey has no
Ends
Still beaten she will challenge
Still hungry she will feast
Today she will believe in her crops
Today she will face her rot
For the festival of tomorrow

She is thanks...

My highest praise go to my ancestors for what I've found I've got.

This goes to love - the men behind my frame, the loves who were joy and male, the knitwork of this unwinding, time-changing, naked and delighted the love that which is given can always be reignited.

Many thanks to Aerron, always, everyday for being the 'control freak', pushing, aiming and keeping focus, for loving and non-judgemental attitudes to work; for the team-work behind the name *Shame* and Michelle Scally Clarke, and for our shared vision over the last seven years and beyond. My thanks to Mark, his partner, who gives us space to believe and dream.

Many thanks to my daughter Olivia, sisters, cousins and God-children, who pushed *she is* to the forefront of my work and written reflections. We are *she is*. Big love to Michelle Jeremiah, Paula White, Lady M, Sammi Powell, Claire, Rebecca and Annie, Chantel Davis, Lisa Clarke, Mirry Shott, Julie Washington, Mel McGrass, Donneilla Bass, Liz Powell, Granny Scally, Auntie Carmel, Fiona Lambert, Paulette and Annette Morris, for the *she is* in our journey.

To my first born, Joseph, my beautiful parents
Michael and Margaret Scally, who are the
substance to my unconditional grounding and
freedom to the free wild poetic spirit.

The deepest sense of thanks and love go to
General and his mother and father who birthed
him to be my friend to the end.

To the people who made this dream possible,
Aerron Perry, Ian Daley, Nicole Zepmeisel, Roisin
O'Shea, The Funky Diva, Andy Campbell. Kevin
and Katie Reynolds. Thank you for being the
root, Route, to my fruit.

But also, this is for you, reflections, for our
emotions everyday, if it touches you then we can
but pass each page to our story, each acceptance
of the road, although it's long and travelled, each
story is pure gold.

She Is - CD*

1. **The cold that let in the rain** (Scally Clarke)
2. **Safe** (Scally Clarke/Perry)
3. **One night stand** (Scally Clarke/Perry/James)
4. **Dear God** (Scally Clarke)
5. **Beautiful** (Scally Clarke)
6. **She is** (Scally Clarke/Perry)
7. **Destiny** (Scally Clarke)
8. **You came** (Scally Clarke/Perry/Emerson)
9. **Letdown** (Scally Clarke/Perry/Emerson)
10. **Today** (Scally Clarke)

All lead and backing vocals – Michelle Scally Clarke
Sequencing, soundscapes and arrangements –
Aerron Perry
Guitar on 'You Came' and 'Letdown'– Steve Emerson

All tracks produced by Aerron Perry except 'One
Night Stand' produced by Aerron Perry and Bryn
James for Turbo Nine Productions
(www.turbonine.com).

Thanks to Bryn James and Steve Emerson for their
input, Ian Daley and Joe Williams for guidance.
Roisin, The Funky Diva, Ricky Venel Stone, Tony
Nicely, Chris Campbell for support. Mark for being
there. Thanks Dean and Toby for listening.

Recorded at Blue Sight, Leeds.

*Copies of this book bought in the UK come with a
free CD. If your book came without a CD, you can
order one from www.route-online.com

Website

For more information on Michelle Scally Clarke please visit her webiste. Pushing poetry into the digital world this site includes:

- Interactive Flash movies of selected poems from *She Is*

- Exclusive audio and video tracks

- Up to the minute tour information

- Michelle's living journal

www.michellescallyclarke.co.uk

Also by Michelle Scally Clarke

I Am

ISBN 1 901927 08 3
£10 Including free CD

At thirty years old, Michelle is the same age as the mother who gave her up into care as a baby. In the quest to find her birth parents, her roots and her own identity, this book traces the journey from care, to adoption, to motherhood, to performer. Using the fragments of her own memory, her poetry and extracts from her adoption files, Michelle rebuilds the picture of 'self' that allows her to transcend adversity and move forward to become the woman she was born to be.

You can hear the beat and song of Michelle Scally Clarke on the CD that accompanies this book and, on the inside pages, read the story that is the source of that song.

'Every now and again individuals comes along who breathe new life into performance poetry. Michelle Scally Clarke is one such individual. Her intelligence, her verbal agility and her passion means that poetry is alive once more.' - **Benjamin Zephaniah**

'Instead of courting on the obvious of the lost community, Michelle looks within, within herself and within us. The strengths and the weaknesses therein.' - **Lemn Sissay**

Order now from www.route-online.com

Psychicbread

Mark Gwynne Jones

ISBN 1 901927 20 2 £6.95

Psychicbread introduces Mark Gwynne Jones and the space between our thoughts. Drawing on an ancient tradition, these captivating and slightly mad, mind altering poems tackle the complexities of our changing world with a beautiful and savage humour. This groundbreaking collection presents the word in print, audio and film, coming complete with a CD of poems and stories - soundscaped, empowered by percussion and projected in a series of compelling films.

Adult Entertainment

Chloe Poems

ISBN 1 901927 18 0 £6.95

One of the most prodigiously gifted and accessible poets alive today, Chloe Poems has been described as 'an extraordinary mixture of Shirley Temple and pornography.' This collection of political and social commentary, first presented in Midsummer 2002, contains twenty-three poems of uncompromising honesty and explicit republicanism, and comes complete with a fourteen track CD of Chloe live in performance.

Half a Pint of Tristram Shandy

Jo Pearson, Daithidh MacEochaidh, Peter Knaggs

ISBN 1 901927 15 6 £6.95

A three-in-one poetry collection from the best in a generation of young poets. Between the leaves of this book lies the mad boundless energy of the globe

cracking-up under our very noses; it is a world
which is harnessed in images of jazz, sex, drugs,
aliens, abuse; in effective colloquial language and
manic syntax; but the themes are always treated
with gravity, unsettling candour and humour.

Moveable Type
Rommi Smith
ISBN 1 901927 11 3 £10 Including free CD
It is the theme of discovery that is at the heart of
Moveable Type. Rommi Smith takes the reader on a
journey through identity, language and memory, via
England and America, with sharp observation, wit
and wry comment en route. *Moveable Type* and its
accompanying CD offer the reader the opportunity to
listen or read, read and listen. Either way, you are
witnessing a sound that is uniquely Rommi Smith.

Jack and Sal

Anthony Cropper,
ISBN 1-901927 21 0 £8.95
Jack and Sal, two people drifting in and out of love.
Jack searches for clues, for a pattern, for an
explanation to life's events. Perhaps the answer is
in evolution, in dopamine, in chaos theory, or maybe
it can be found in the minutiae of domesticity where
the majority of life's dramas unfold. Here, Anthony
Cropper has produced a delicately detailed account
of a troubled relationship, with a series of micro-
stories and incidents that recount the intimate lies,
loves and lives of Jack and Sal and their close
friend Paula.

Next Stop Hope - Route 14

Ed. M Y Alam, Anthony Cropper, Ian Daley
ISBN 1-901927 19 9 £6.95
A title in the route series, presented in three
distinct collections: *Criminally Minded*, *Something
Has Gone Wrong in the World* and *Next Stop Hope*.
This anthology of new writing takes you skilfully
through the inner workings of the criminal mind,
the nuances of human relationships and our
personal connections with an increasingly
disturbing world, where hope is hard to find.
Featuring new short fiction and poetry from thirty-
three writers including M Y Alam, Val Cale, Anthony
Cropper, Susan Everett, Mark Gwynne Jones,
Daithidh MacEochaidh, Jo Pearson, Chloe Poems,
Michelle Scally Clarke and Adrian Wilson.

Warehouse

MS Green, Alan Green, Clayton Devanny, Simon Nodder, Jono Bell - Ed Ian Daley

ISBN 1-901927 10 5 £6.95

Warehouse is a unique type of social realism, written by young warehouse operatives from the bottom end of the labour market in the middle of the post-industrial heartland, it steps to the beat of modern day working-class life. A soundtrack to the stories is included on a complimentary CD, warehouse blues supplied by *The Chapter* and urban funk grooves from *Budists*

One Northern Soul

J R Endeacott

ISBN 1-901927 17 2 - £5.95

If that goal in Paris had been allowed then everything that followed could have been different. For young Stephen Bottomley something died that night. *One Northern Soul* follows the fortunes of this Leeds United fan as he comes of age in the dark days of the early eighties.

Kilo

M Y Alam

ISBN 1-901927 09 1 - £6.95

Khalil Khan had a certain past and an equally certain future awaited until gangsters decided to turn his world upside down. They shattered his safe family life with baseball bats but that's just the beginning. They turned good, innocent and honest Khalil into someone else: Kilo, a much more unforgiving and determined piece of work. Kilo cuts his way through the underworld of Bradford street crime, but the closer he gets to the top of that game, the stronger the pull of his original values become.

The Blackstuff
Val Cale
ISBN 1-901927 14 8 £6.95
The Blackstuff is a true story of a road-trip that
sees Val Cale in trouble in Japan, impaled in Nepal,
ripped off at a vaginal freak show in Bangkok,
nearly saturated by a masturbating Himalayan bear
in the most southerly town of India and culminates
in a mad tramp across the world looking for the
ultimate blowjob and the meaning of life.

Very Acme
Adrian Wilson
ISBN: 1 901927 12 1 £6.95
New Nomad, nappy expert, small town man and
ultimately a hologram – these are the life roles of
Adrian Wilson, hero and author of this book, which
when he began writing it, was to become the world's
first novel about two and a half streets. All this
changes when a new job sends him all around the
world. *Very Acme* is about small town life in the
global age and trying to keep a sense of identity in a
world of multi-corporations and information
overload.

Like A Dog To Its Vomit
Daithidh MacEochaidh
ISBN:1901927 07 5 £6.95
In this complex, stylish and downright dirty novel,
Daithidh MacEochaidh belts through the underclass
underachieving postponed-modern sacrilege and the
more pungent bodily orifices. *Like a Dog to Its Vomit*
is a must read for anyone who has ever poked their
weary toe into the world of critical theory, many of
the postmodern textual games and strategies are on
offer, used, abused, open to derision, and yet
strangely sanctioned in the end.

Crazy Horse
Susan Everett
ISBN 1 901927 06 7 £6.95

Jenny Barker, like many young women, has a few
problems. She is trying to get on with her life, but it
isn't easy. Her beloved horse has been stolen while
the vicious *Savager* is on the loose cutting up
animals in fields. She's neither doing well in college
nor in love and fears she may die a virgin.

For more details on all these titles,
to buy books and to download
new writing please visit

www.route-online.com